T0196894

GROWING UP
IN CHRIST
AND THE
World

EVANGELIST JANICE L. MCCOY

WESTBOW
PRESS®
A DIVISION OF THOMAS NELSON
& ZONDERVAN

WestBow Press books may be ordered through
booksellers or by contacting:

WestBow Press
A Division of Thomas Nelson & Zondervan
1663 Liberty Drive
Bloomington, IN 47403
www.westbowpress.com
1 (866) 928-1240

ISBN: 978-1-5127-6731-5 (sc)
ISBN: 978-1-5127-6730-8 (e)

Library of Congress Control Number: 2016920235

Print information available on the last page.

WestBow Press rev. date: 12/12/2016

If you are divorced and have been saved, the blood of Jesus has washed your sins away and you are clean. None of your sins or divorce are held against you. They no longer exist. In this study, and when studying the Bible, always check to understand what covenant is in place where you are. Be blessed, and remember your sins are gone, no more, not covered by the blood of lambs and goats but washed by the blood of Jesus.

CONTENTS

PREFACE

This is not a book that you can read and understand it. It is a deeper study and must be prayed about and illuminated by the Holy Spirit. I have not written this to be a best seller but to inform and so it can be used as a learning tool for those interested in going deeper with the Lord. I don't really know why it is important to be written but maybe it is for only one person. Remember—if it makes sense, it doesn't usually make faith. I cannot give you the revelation, but I can say you must have revelation to understand the new covenant. I pray you will get all God has meant for you to have and at the same time get understanding. May God bless you as you read and study.

Chapter 1

Moving from Glory to Glory

From beginning to end, how do I grow and mature in the Lord? I was told that once I grew up, I'd have to be grown for the rest of my life, so I decided I'd wait to grow up. Your body can age, get tall, or grow fat, but maturing is a choice.

Have you ever seen old men wearing crazy stuff that doesn't fit their age? Old ladies do the same thing. It looks silly but is so sad. Either they've learned nothing about style, want to stand out, or don't care. What is appropriate for the young is not always good for the old. Maturing in Christ is another choice. Before I came back to the Lord, I believed we had a fifty-fifty chance of making the right choice or decision, but that is simply not true.

The choices are not fifty-fifty—they are more like six to one in favor of missing the mark.

For example, standing in the middle of a one-lane road with a truck coming, we may choose to do nothing, take a step back, step to the left, step to the right, step forward, or get out of the road. Five choices will get us run over. Only if we make the right choice—get out of the road—will we escape injury.

You have one choice.

So it is with the Word of God. We have a choice to believe it, read it, do it. But others we are listening to—including preachers or church leaders—may be wrong. The responsibility is on us—not them, *us*. I have nothing against ministers, but we need to study up. We must know what the Bible says, or at least when we hear something, we must look it up. I would rather be responsible for my own soul. Wrong beliefs can cause us to miss heaven.

Only we can open our minds to new revelation. We must *do* each thing—first believe it, second read it, and third do it by acting on what we believe. The Bible interprets itself, so until we read it through and through, we can't understand. It's a mystery.

Do we love our children? Are we willing to *die* for them to have salvation? Most aren't, or they would die for Christ so their children, through their walk with Christ, would be blessed.

The covenant is a family guarantee from the Savior. The Passover in Egypt proves that not only the family but also the servants and the flocks were saved. This covenant was lambs' blood, an old covenant. The directions are given in the Bible, and if we have not prayed, studied, and started again when our answer has not manifested, we are stuck with a religion that does not work. If things are not working, we must realize we have missed them, for God has not changed. Religion does not work. If we see someone else causing us to miss the message, *look*—it's us! We are the reason we missed it!

This is not an easy book to write, for it will indeed make many free. I was called to preach in 1963, on fire for God, but when I started reading the book and listening to men of God I respected, I was so discouraged that I fell away for twenty-seven years. I felt bound by sin for all I had done for all my life and was always reminded of it by family and friends. My sins were washed away by the blood of Jesus Christ on the very day I asked forgiveness. Finally, God put me in front of a godly woman. Although

I have told her how much she means to me, I am sure she could have no idea of how much she really does mean to me. She has been so abused by so-called Christians because she didn't have much in worldly goods and had no special clothes to wear to church. With a little sick child and two other children, she showed up to a Pentecostal church and could hear the whispers as she went to the altar and wept through the entire service, but there was no one to help the pain except Jesus; He was enough. Do you claim to be Spirit-filled and have this same kind of fruit?

Many people call themselves Pentecostal because they belong to a denomination, and others believe they are Pentecostal, but many have missed the mark. Pentecostalism is an experience beyond the mortal imagination, and even once we have it, it should be renewed and refined daily in a closer walk with Him through reading and hearing His Word. Though sometimes we get or have goose bumps in the flesh, the actual experience is only the beginning of a secure walk and relationship with the Father. Too many settle for far too little for too long. We go to the altar, get that good feeling, and go home until the next service, and then we come again and again for the good feeling for which we settle.

I don't mean to be unkind, but I ask myself what John the Baptist would say. What would Jesus think? He walked into the temple and turned over the pews. My Father's house is a house of prayer. Remember: they were under the law. I have been told I am too harsh, but they didn't approve of Jesus or John the Baptist. Telling the truth doesn't seem mean or harsh to me.

The religious of that day condemned sinners. They—not Christians but people who think they are Christians—still do condemn sinners, but Jesus never did. Always forgiving and loving, His blood restored us to righteousness. Once my spiritual mother and I were discussing how blessed I was, and she said, "Someone prayed for you." It was like a spear in my heart—those words pierced so deeply. No one was left praying for my children and grandchildren. I had never met anyone who could get a prayer answered. I went to my room, fell on my knees, started praying in tongues, and said to God, "Please, don't let it be too late." I knew I deserved hell and was going there, but I didn't want my children to go there. *No, not them!*

As I prayed, I began to tell God all the stupid stuff I learned in church—stupid because it simply didn't work, some truths, some half-truths. But there is no lying to God—He knows what you are thinking, so there is no need to play games. He is all knowing, all hearing, and all seeing. He is! In the morning when I came out of the room, my friend said she had never seen such a change in a person. I seemed to be a person she had never known before. This is what I want you to learn from this book.

First and foremost, you must simply pray for the revelation of your death, your spiritual death to Christ. You must learn to live in the spiritual realm, which is the real world. The Word says that to live we must die to self. You need to decide to have all or nothing at all. To enjoy and live in this life you must entirely be dead to self. I'm still working on it. It seems this natural man wants to keep rising up to live. With prayer and Revelation you will be living larger than life. So totally give whatever He asks, no matter how silly it sounds, for He uses the silly things of this world to confound the wise. You must decide to follow Him only—no in-betweens or you will get discouraged and fall away. You must begin to see all problems, trouble, and difficulties as a way to move up in your walk. The Word says we move from glory to glory, but it seems like trouble to trouble. You will begin to see—with spiritual eyes—when you have a problem, and if you praise, the problem will pass faster. Remember: He said,

"It came to pass," not, "It came to stay." You must realize you have a problem, and then you must start praising. Only then will you begin to see the problem passing.

Brother John Hagee Sr. has a terrific series called *Problem, Provision, and Promise.* It has twelve tapes, and I believe if you will listen to the teaching, you will hear it with spiritual ears. Begin to play your Bible tapes all day and all night. Ask the Holy Spirit to teach you the Word and show you the truth. When it falls into your spirit, you will know and understand what I mean. If you only hear with your ears, you will miss what He has for you. You must desire the entirety of what Jesus died for. We don't deserve anything, but Jesus deserves we get the very best. We can't have just the part we want— we must have it all!

I saw myself on the cross and felt the pain in my side. I saw myself go through the gates of heaven and knew I was in the kingdom of God. Not later— now. When this body falls off, I will just change locations, and He will give me a glorified body. Of course, we will get stuff in heaven, but victory and blessings are for this life. Our armor is for this life. There will be no fighting in heaven. Abundance is for this life, not a pie in the sky. When we die, nothing should change but our location. Jesus died for us to have everything here.

Let us go back to the beginning. Genesis is not the beginning, for before that God was standing on nothing on the corner of nowhere. God may have said or decided to make a type of planet called heaven. The Word says He knew us before the foundation of the world. Get this in your mind. He knew us then. Some like to say you existed before. Don't get bogged down in a futile unprovable theory. Just say, "It says He knew me somehow. I don't know how. He planned for me to have everything, and it is taken care of." By grace we are saved, not of ourselves. We were chosen before the beginning, and Jesus knew me before the beginning and Christ was crucified before the beginning. Think about how much more grace is than what we think. We must remember this—when truth hits and we see (with our spiritual eyes), it is fixed, already taken care of. No problem, stay when you see this. Just praise for the victory no matter what it looks like with our natural eyes. We walk by faith, not by sight. He made many different kinds of beings, angels, etc. Lucifer was the most beautiful and most powerful and even was the glory holder and the lead worshipper with all the musical instruments. Then they (Father, Son, and Holy

Spirit) decided to create an earth and creatures on it, with light, all fresh, new, and beautiful. (It is Genesis 1:1, perfect in all its beauty.) They put Lucifer over this kingdom to bring them (Father, Son, and Holy Spirit) praises of the inhabitants of the earth. According to the Word, Lucifer wanted the praise and caused war in heavens and the calamity came, according to Job. The earth and skies collapsed and were in the darkness. This is the first destruction. Now they (Father, Son, Holy Spirit) decided to make man and to make him in His image so that He could have children. All the beings in heaven do not make God as happy as one child who has chosen to love Him, hence *"re-creation"* (Gen. 1:2). After seven days, and man was to replenish the earth and have dominion over it. He created them. Now some don't believe this theory so don't get bogged down with move on.

Most of us know that after a while God made Eve, whom He called "Adam" also. Satan deceived her, and Adam allowed it and Adam gave his dominion to Satan. Then Adam and Eve were cast out of Eden (the spot where God is). You can read this story in your Bible. The people multiplied and were scattered on earth, and Satan sent his fallen angels from the mountains and mixed their blood with that of men to mix all blood so Jesus could not be born. *But* God found a man named Noah *who* was in right standing with God and warned him of the coming flood. Noah preached the coming of the flood and began to build a boat in the middle of the desert. Try to picture this in your mind. It had never rained on the earth, so would *you* have believed Noah (a man of four to five hundred years of age)? He preached the flood for 150 years, and then all the animals loaded themselves two by two and four by four onto the ark, then Noah and his family. Still no rain. God sealed the door. Note: the ark was a type and shadow of Christ. Noah's entire family was saved, although *only* Noah was found right with God. (Did you get that?) A lamb for a household. Then we had the flood! When you saw with your eyes all those animals getting on board, do you think you would have believed and gotten on board? It is in this day. We may say, "I am not stupid or dumb. I would not have done what Adam did." We are still doing what they did! Maybe you say, "Oh, I have tomorrow." Satan's big lie is that you have tomorrow. No you don't, and even if you happen to have tomorrow, your child may not! What about them? Yes, are you going to play church or not even go to church? Do you miss services? You have crippled the body of Christ, no matter how unimportant you may think you are. Even if you are the little toe, how well does a body walk without a toe? Pay attention here, folks. God is telling us something we don't want to hear, but we are going to be accountable for every word spoken, every unkindness, every unforgiveness. If someone has done something bad to you, you better ask *him or her* to forgive you and get right with God. He and His thoughts about you are all that are important. You are *called* by God to be a King/Priest to Him. Most have none of His gifts nor want them. You can't imagine the wonderfulness of His presence, His gifts, and all His "stuff" He has for us right here on earth. Now you are in the kingdom of God! Now you have victory in Jesus. Now is when you need to use your armor for the Word of God. God has not created you to wait to get to heaven to live with and be for Him but desires to be with you and in your presence now—to live and move in you. But most of us only mention Him in passing one or twice weekly or Christmas and Easter! Jesus was crucified! He is not a babe in a manger. He is not a beaten Christ. He is not on the cross or in the grave! *He is the risen King of Kings, Lord of Lords who sits on the right hand of God, interceding for me and you (if you want). He gave us* power and dominion over all things, but to use it we must walk constantly with Him and in Him and in His presence, forsaking all else. His desire is to have His good pleasure in us. He desires us to be

11

holy. We must desire to know *Him* as intimately as we know our wife or husband. Under the heading of *dominion and power are* other words for power and authority, which I will speak of now. First realize the dominion and authority were given to the church, which is you and me, not men. Paul tells us in Christ we are all the same. There is no distinction between us as far as God is concerned.

We must have the mind of Christ. In the kingdom, there is no respecter of persons. I shared the fact with a really faithful and religious preacher's wife (whom I respected a lot). I shared the fact that I don't cry on my knees to God four or five hours a day. The Bible told me to "pray always in all ways," and that is what I do. I pray all the time, standing, sitting and just talking to my Lord—a continual prayer and/or conversation to heaven (similar to breathing). She said it didn't mean that. I never break connection to my Father, for He is in me. If I could scrape the skin back, you would see Him. At times, I just stop everything and wait on Him and listen for Him. Sometimes I fall asleep waiting. Pray without ceasing every moment. Every day is a Sabbath to me. His very presence is upon me, in me, and around me. He has manifested His presence so many different ways for healing. I would never have believed there were so many ways for people to receive their healing. I will share the healings after I thoroughly "rinse" you with dominion.

If the Word does not seem to be working for you, try this. Change something—the way you live, the way you pray, the way you study your Bible. The Word always works. My expression is, "The Word can't work unless we work the Word." Too many times we keep doing the same things over and over again expecting a different result.

CHAPTER 2

Dominion

You must understand what a blood covenant is to be aware of your standing. Jesus was our sacrifice—our blood sacrifice, once and for all. He finished the work, and there is nothing left for us to do but walk in it as He did. To the victor belongs the spoils, and Jesus was victorious over death, hell, the grave, and the devil, and He gives us the *power* (authority) to use His name. My pastor once told me a victor sends in his army, and then when they win, he goes and gets the "spoils" (jewelry, flock, etc.). The Word says we are more than conquerors. All we have to do is get our spoils. How? By using the Word. A blood covenant is unbreakable. We have become a nation of covenant breakers. Even heathens in other nations will respect a blood covenant between their fathers down through the generations. Our word is no longer of any report. We do not do what we say or say what we will do. Therefore, we don't believe God told the truth and we have a problem believing Him. It is because we are liars, and we think He is too. A blood covenant can be a formal ritual between two persons when they marry. The hymen is broken and they are covenanted together, and through their children they become one. That child is them in one. If a covenant breaking occurs, the child is spiritually ripped apart. We have not seen this or taught this and wonder why divorce is so hard on the children. They are no longer whole but ripped and should be prayed back together and anointed In the old temple, the priest made the sacrifice and sat down at the third hour and said, "It is finished," just as Jesus hung on the cross and said, "It is finished." The sacrifice and all the work was *done*! (Not meaning the crucifixion is over but that *all the work was finished*! Not to be continued—nothing for anyone else to do.)

For example, if you build a car and finish it, all you have to do is drive. You don't need to continue building. So is the kingdom of God. It is finished. All you have to do is grab hold of the truths of the Word and go with it. Stand on it, quote it, and do it. The problem is people make a covenant with the Father, get baptized and maybe even Spirit-filled, and stop. You will have problems anyway! Why not use them to move up in your walk with God? It is finished/drive the car. Grow up in *Christ*.

Your dominion will come a little at a time as you can handle the power. God is not going to allow you to rain down fire from heaven until you will only use wisely. Or you may be spewing fire on people who make you angry. Or maybe if God allowed you to rain down hail, you would do it to someone who had did something to you. The Word says you have the power to forgive sin just as Jesus did. That is why it says to forgive those who would do you harm. Those you forgive are forgiven etc., (Wow, did I say that?) Look it up! It is there, it is in the "seeking you will find." The *only* thing we are allowed to do is seek Him, allow His will in us, and allow Him to produce the fruit. By the way, the fruit of the Spirit can only be produced by the Holy Spirit as the vine and we are the branch. We are only part of the vine and dependent on the vine, *so* either you have the fruit or you don't.

You cannot have Him and not have the fruit. Remember, Jesus was under the law. Look at what you are reading. See if it was under the law or under the new covenant. Even in New Testament some stuff is written under the law.

Back to dominion. I always suggest to our people to begin with Mathew, Mark, Luke, and John and read the *red*. Jesus said the *red* ... Do what He did! Just start. Say, "Jesus, forgive me. Come into my heart. Give me fire for your Word." Then I suggest reading each book six times to begin with. The more you read, the faster you read, the quicker He can teach you. Put aside old rituals and hearsays, stuff some preachers may have said. You may have heard him wrong. Start *doing* for Jesus, right now, where you are. Hear what He is saying to you. Stop trying to be religious and/or trying to please people. Jesus loves you just as you are and for what you can become in Him. Always be willing to take the time to tell someone about Him. Believe me, He will give you many opportunities to do it, and it will never be at a convenient time and/or you may not even feel up to the job. Don't miss this chance because you will not *only* miss your blessing but He may send someone else. Always drop *everything* for a chance to tell anyone about Him. He is like any other Father. He loves for His kids to brag about Him. Always remember, what He sees in secret, He will reward you openly. When I first meet a person and may have only one encounter with him or her, I always suggest he or she begin with Mathew, Mark, Luke, and John and go through these four books before he or she continues on with the Word. This is what Jesus did, and He is our example. If we just begin to say and do and act as Jesus did, we cannot be deterred from our faith and our walk. It is important to get enough of Him and what He was like here on earth that we quit depending on what people say we need to do. The Holy Spirit is our teacher, and He alone can teach us without error *if* we pay attention and become obedient, remembering Jesus was a Jew and always under the old covenant until His resurrection. From Acts to Revelation, we are sealed with the Holy Spirit and are no longer under the law, any of it—not even the Ten Commandments.

We are made alive by the Spirit "Even when we were dead in sins, hath quickened us together with Christ, by grace you are saved." (Ephesians 1:5) continue Ephesians.

Chapter 3

New Covenant

*T*here is nothing *new* under the sun. What we call *new* is new knowledge to us. A new level in Christ is growth by growing up in the Word, for there is nothing *new* under the sun. The Word is the same and unchanging, but as we grow up in Christ, we receive *new* levels or revelation and more knowledge as we can understand it. Our walk with Christ *must* overcome our "religion," for doctrines of men or churches will nullify and void our walk with Christ, for when *He* tries to show us a *new* thing and we refuse it, we can no longer receive till we are ready to believe *Him* (the Holy Spirit). Just because we believe something doesn't change the truth. The Bible is a mystery, and only true revelation must come from God. You can believe there is no such thing as electricity. Before it was discovered, no one knew it was there. That did not mean it was not there all the time and we still can't see it, but unless we believe it, anyway but we will never have lights unless we tap into it. The New Covenant is not an extension of the Old Covenant. There must have been an Old Covenant or there would be no need to call it a New Covenant. If the Old Covenant was better, there would have been no need for the New Covenant. We need to work harder at letting go of tradition and allow the Holy Spirit to do a *new* work in us. It is *not new* but is new to us because we now understand it. It is *new* to *me* or *new* to you. I am not going to get deep into the Old Covenant, for you can study it for yourself. Realize what the Old Covenant was about. *Do not hold onto* any of it, for it is not possible to keep. If it had been possible to keep, there would be no need for a *new* and *better covenant.* Man will tell you the Ten Commandments are relevant but only to a sinner for him to know he is a sinner. A Christian has been reclaimed and is no longer under the law. We must understand what the Old Covenant is.

> "For where a testament (last will and testament) is, there must also be the death of the testator. For a testament is enforced after men are dead:

otherwise it is of no strength at all while the testator lives. Whereupon neither the first testament was dedicated without blood. For when Moses had spoken every precept to all the people according to the law, he took the blood of calves and of goats with water and scarlet wool and hyssop, and sprinkled both the book, and all the people saying, *this* is the blood of the testament which God hath enjoined unto you. Moreover, he sprinkled with blood both the tabernacle and all the vessels of the ministry."(Hebrews 9:16–25)

The New Testament *is* our inheritance. It is the same as when your parents die and you read the will and receive the things (money, jewelry, etc.) they have left you in the will. Same it is with the New Testament. It was not in effect until after Jesus's death. Mathew, Mark, Luke, and John are still *Old* Covenant because Jesus had not died yet. Many, most actually, have never read their will, their inheritance, but have depended on others to read it to them a dab at a time. If your earthly father were to leave you a vast fortune, would you be satisfied to hear an attorney say, "Your parents only left you $3,000"? Or would you say, "Let me see that!" This is what most people do, even Christians. Many times we settle for a small amount when God said He gave you all things. "And almost all things are by the law purged with blood, and without shedding of blood is no remission of sins."(John 3:25, Matthew 26:26, Hebrews 9:22)

It was therefore necessary that the patterns of things in the heavens should be purified with these—but the heavenly things themselves with better sacrifices than these. For Christ is not entered into the holy place made with hands, which are the figures of the truth, but into heaven itself, now to appear in the presence of God for us, nor that he should offer Himself often as the high priest enters into the holy place every year with blood of others. Hebrews 9:28 says, "So Christ was once offered to bear the sins of many, and unto them that look for (look for, look for, are you looking?) Him shall He appear the second time without sin unto salvation."

> To declare I say, at this time His righteousness: that He might be just, and the justifier of him which believeth in Jesus [giving us His righteousness]. Where is boasting then? It is excluded. By what law? of

works? Nay: but by the *law of faith.* Therefore, we conclude that a man is justified by faith without the deeds of the law. [We are His righteousness without doing anything.] (Romans 3:26–31)

I was told I was sealed with the Sabbath day but the Bible clearly states "I am sealed with the Holy Spirit" (2 Corinthians 1:22, Ephesians 1:13)

For it is not possible that the blood of bulls and of goats should take away sins. ... For there is verily a disannulling of the commandment going before for the weakness and unprofitable thereof. For the law made nothing perfect, but the bringing in of a better hope did; by which we draw near unto God. (Hebrews 10:4, 7:18–19)

Because the law works wrath: for where no law is, there is no transgression. Therefore it is of faith, that it might be by grace, to the end the promise might be sure to all the seed; not to that only which is of the law, but to that also which is of the faith of Abraham; who is the father of us all. (Romans 4:15–16)

There was no law before the Abrahamic Covenant, yet Noah sacrificed after the flood and Abraham tithed to Melchizedec before the law also. God gave the law so we could see we were sinners, but the new Covenant release us from the law because we are *one* with Him.

Be it known unto you therefore, men and brethren, that through this man is preached unto you the forgiveness of sins: And by Him all that believe are justified from all things, from which ye could not be justified by the law of Moses. Beware therefore, lest that come upon you, which is spoken of in the prophets; Behold, ye despisers, and wonders and perish: for I work a work in you which ye shall in no wise believe, though a man declares it unto you. (Acts 13:38–41)

The Old Covenant was given to Abraham (Abram) but was called the Law of Moses. He put it on paper. It was God's way back into the earth. After Noah, God had no man on earth. God must abide by his own laws, and without a body there is no authority on earth. That is why Satan is always trying to possess a body. You must have a body to be legal on earth and have dominion. That's why all those demons wanted to go into the pigs. They want bodies, and we need to be sure they don't use ours.

> But I see another law in my members, warring against the law of my mind, and bringing me into captivity to the law of sin which is in my member [body]. … For the law of the Spirit of Life in Christ Jesus hath made me *free from the law of sin and death.* [Man's law versus Moses's law; read *all* of Romans.] (Romans 7:23, 8:2)

> For when we were in the flesh, the motion of sins, which were by the law, did work in our members to bring forth fruit not death. But now we are delivered from the law, that being dead wherein we were held; that we should serve in newness of

spirit, and not in the oldness of the letter. (Romans 7:5–6)

And the Law is not of faith: but the man that doeth them shall live in them. Christ Hath redeemed us from the curse of the law, being made a curse for us. (Galatians 3:12)

Read Galatians 3–5, 10. We must walk in faith, for without it we cannot please God.

Stand fast therefore in Liberty wherewith Christ hath made us free, and be not entangled again with the Yoke of bondage. (Galatians 5:1)

Christians have been held in bondage due to a divorce, yet murderers have been freed by the same Christians. Whom the Son has freed is free indeed! What part of, "It is finished" do we not understand? Jesus said, "It is finished," *not,* "To be *continued by someone else.*"

It is finished.

For Christ is the end of the law for righteousness to everyone that believeth. (Romans 10:4)

We are in Him because of Him.

How was it under the law? In the beginning …

> When man hath taken a wife, and married her, and it come to pass that she found no favor in his eyes, because he has found some uncleanness in her: then let him write her bill of divorcement, and give it in her hand, and send her out of his house. And when she is departed out of his house, she may go and be another man's wife. And if the latter husband hate her, and write her a bill of divorcement, and giveth it in her hand and sends her out of his house, or if the latter husband die, which took her to be his wife, her former husband, which sent her away, may not take her again to be his wife, after that she is defiled (she is only defiled to him, for he put her away for that is abomination before the Lord); and thou shalt not cause the land to sin, which the Lord thy God giveth thee for an inheritance. (Deuteronomy 24:1–4)

Matthew 5:31–32 says, "It hath said, Whomsoever shall put away his wife, let him give her a writing of divorcement." Jesus is under the Law—not resurrected. He is quoting the law back to the law keepers. They already knew the law and were expert in it. Verse 32 is law. Put away (*appoluo*=to loose) is to set at liberty.

Put away was divorce and understood by Jews. If the divorce was granted for fornication, a sin God looked upon as most serious, the putting away was legal, sanctioned by Christ. It made the contract null and void (Dake's Annotated Reference Bible) as before marriage, covered by sheep's blood. How much more does Jesus's blood do?

Some preachers claim you cannot free yourself from the sin of divorce. They are in error. The divorced person is set at liberty, for the blood of Jesus *washes white as snow,* as though you have never sinned.

Deuteronomy 24:1–4 talks about legal document dissolving the marriage bonds. It is called a 'writing of divorcement *law* (Jeremiah 3:8). Mark 10:4 says, "And they said, Moses suffered to write a bill of divorcement, and to put her away" (loose or free her). See also Mark 10:2–4.

In Mark 10:7–12, tempting Him (Jesus) is still under the law. The question here is not the right to remarry but only the right to divorce. The Pharisee wanted to know which side of the controversy Jesus was on. It was custom to divorce and remarry times without number. He did not change the Jewish universal practice that a right to divorce was a right to remarriage. He let this be as it was in Deuteronomy 24:1–4:

> When a man hath taken a wife, and married her, and it comes to pass that she found no favor in his eyes because he hath found some uncleanness in her: then let him write her a bill of divorcement, and give it in her hand, and send her out of his house. And when she is departed out of his house, she may go and be another man's wife. And if the latter husband hates her and write her a bill of divorcement and giveth it in her hand, and sends her out of his house; or if the latter husband die, which took her to be his wife. Her former husband, which send her away, may *not* take her again to be his wife, after that she is defiled; for that

is abomination before the Lord and
thou shalt not cause the land to sin,
which the Lord thy God giveth thee
for an inheritance.

There was the Old Covenant tradition: "An ancient Jewish bill of divorce reads thus 'on the ---day of the week---day of the month---in the year---who am also called the son of ---of the city of---by the river of---do hereby consent with my one will, being under no restraint, and do hereby release, send away, and put aside thee, my wife---who is also called the daughter of---who are this day in the city of---by the river of---who has been my wife in time pass; and thus I do release thee, and send thee away and put thee aside that thou may have permission and control over thyself to go to be married to any man that thou may desire; and that no man shall hinder thee from this day forward, and thou are permitted to any man, and this shall be unto thee from me a bill of dismissal, a document of release, and a letter of freedom, according to the law of Moses and Israel'" (Dake's Annotated Reference Bible).

Answer on Divorcement

Matthew 5:31–32 (Old Covenant) and 19:1–8 were given to *non*-Christians and for all men in general. A Christian is a new creature in Christ and a true imitator of Jesus in life. Christians are born again and filled with the Spirit. This is not a person just saying he or she is a Christian, believing he or she is a Christian by joining a church, or believing in God or just saying so but a true praise and worshipper of God. Christians are people who have died so Christ may live, work, and reign in their bodies.

Matthew 5:17–18 says we are not to come under the law. He came to fulfill what was *not fulfilled* till the crucifixion and then gave the *new commandment*. *Love*—if you love your neighbor, you will not want to talk, backbite, steal from him, kill him, not love him, etc. You will not do the works of the flesh, for we walk by faith, not by sight.

> For the law made nothing perfect, but the bringing in of a better hope did; by which we draw nigh unto God. (Hebrews 7:19)

> For it is not possible that the blood of
> bulls and of goats should take away
> sins. (Hebrews 10:4)

Sins were only covered under the law, so the
sacrifice had to be done over and over each year.

> Neither by the blood of goats and
> calves, but by *his own blood he* entered
> once into the Holy Place, having
> obtained *eternal* redemption for *us*.
> [You and me. *Hallelujah! Can I get an
> amen!]* For if the blood of bulls and
> of goats, and the ashes of an heifer
> sprinkling the unclean, sanctifies to
> the purifying of the flesh: how much
> more shall the blood of Christ, who
> through the eternal Spirit offered
> Himself without spot to God, purge
> your conscience from dead works
> to serve the living God? (Hebrews
> 9:12–13)

What part of *His blood* did not cleanse us from *all*
sin? What part, and how are *we* supposed to finish
His work? Pray tell—*it is finished*!

The past is washed away, but Satan and his minions want us to stay condemned. For twenty-seven years I was away from my beloved Savior, thinking I was the lowest person in the world and unable in any way for God to use me or even save me from the sin of divorce. That leaves people hopeless and the blood nullified for the divorces and all who have been taught that you need to clean up your act before coming to *Him*. He is the changer. He says come as you are and if you fall He'll pick you up.

Remember in the Old Testament where Abraham laid with the other woman and had the child called Ishmael? In the New Testament he was called a man of great faith, but it sure sounded to me like he didn't have great faith to have his own son by his wife when God said it. *But he was only covered by the blood of goats!* What a better covenant we have. *Washed in the blood of Jesus!*

Yea and amen!

All you need is great faith, all heaven is at your disposal. *Use it.* Faith is a fruit of the Spirit or a gift of faith. All come from the Father. It is a done deal.

Walk in it. Even the Jews (God's chosen people recognized divorce and remarriage) understood the covenant ability to cover sin. Covenant Jesus washes sin away. It is as though you are a virgin all over again. Clean.

> But in those sacrifices [bulls, lambs, etc.] there is a remembrance again made of sin every year." (Hebrews 10:3)

Earthly Sanctuary

In Hebrews 9:1–11, read about the earthly sanctuary: "Then verily the first covenant had also ordinances of divine, and civic and earthly sanctuary."

> For the promise, that he should be the heir of the world, was not to Abraham, or to his seed, through the law, but through the righteousness of faith. For if they which are of the law be heirs, faith is made void, and the promise made of none effect. Because the law works wrath: for where no law is, there is no transgression. So it is of faith, in that it might be by grace; to the end the promise might be sure to all the seed: not to that only which is of the law, etc. (Romans 4:13–16)

Remember this always: a covenant cannot be broken (only by man). God is true and cannot break His part of the bargain (covenant). Every covenant He made He has kept and will keep. Even though Israel broke the covenant with God time and time again, that was a promise made to Abraham, Isaac, and Jacob. God has not wavered from the promises. They are yea and amen. He made a better covenant, and they can accept it and become sons of God because Israel under the law were servants. Now, we may be sons. Allow me to add here: if we stay children, we are still in a type of bondage, due to the fact we have overseers as babysitters as dear children. It is important to grow up. Do not lean only on the words of your pastor. (Pastors can be wrong.) But be confident in what God tells us in His Word. The Holy Spirit will teach and show you, if you allow Him. But you must be grounded firmly in the Word. Get under a Bible-believing Pastor, and allow him to help teach you. And for heaven's sake—your sake—grow up. Stop looking for a word from somebody. Most of our revelation comes directly from the Bible and reading it—not angels or people but His Word *only*.

For more differences between the old and new law:

2 Corinthians 3:14 vs. 2 Corinthians 3:6

Hebrews 8:7; 9:1 vs. Hebrews 10:1–9

2 Corinthians 3:7–14 vs. 2 Corinthians 3:11

Romans 7:12 vs. Hebrews 7:22; 8:6

Hebrews 9:14

Hebrews 8:13 vs. 2 Corinthians 3:6

Hebrews 9:9–10 vs. 2 Corinthians 3:6, 8

2 Corinthians 3:7 vs. 2 Corinthians 3:6,8

Hebrews 9:16–22 vs. Matthew 26:28

Romans 3:26–31 vs. John 1:17

Hebrews 10:4 vs. Galatians 3:13; Hebrews 9:12–15

Hosea 2:11 vs. Hebrews 8:7

Hebrews 9:10–13 vs. 2 Corinthians 3:6, 18

Hebrews 10:2–4 vs. Hebrews 5:9; 10:10

Hebrews 7:19 vs. Hebrews 10:14

2 Corinthians 3:14 vs. 2 Corinthians 3:6

Hebrews 8:7; 9:1 vs. Hebrews 9:7; 10:1–9

John 1:17 vs. Hebrews 8:6; 9:15

Law of Sin

There are many other verses that contrast the Old Law and New Covenant.

> But we know that the law is good, if a man use it lawfully. Knowing this, are you righteous through Christ? That the law is not made for a righteous man, but the law was made for the lawless and disobedient, for the ungodly and for sinners, for unholy and profane, for murderers of fathers and murderers of mothers, for manslayers. For whoremongers, for them that defile themselves with mankind, for men stealers, for liars, for perjured persons and IF there be another thing that is contrary to sound doctrine. (1 Timothy 1:8–10)

New Supersedes Old

Here I must explain sin. Too many do *not* understand *sin* in the eyes of God. The word and religion have confused the issues. The Word says anything *not of faith* is sin. Man has created levels of sin—for instance, drinking is worse than smoking, lying is worse than something else, adultery a little worse than stealing, murder is worse than abortion or the same, and divorce is worse than any of them. But I would like to present to you that we are sinners because we are born into sin. No sin is greater or lesser, but sin is sin in the eyes of God. We have a free will to choose God or we are going to hell. We are now living in eternal life. Everyone will live somewhere forever. This is the time to choose. It's free, and it is the Holy Spirit that gets us where we need to be, but it is by yielding to Him. We begin today. Are you sure you have not missed God?

He loves you so very much if you were the only person alive or to ever have lived, He would have died on that cross for only you. You are so special and unique. There is no one like you and no one who can do what you were put here to do. Take the blessing of a new life today. *Free.* I tried that old life and it was not good. Jesus is the life and the *only* way, my friend.

The New Covenant requires you to be born again (John 9:34). When we think of sin, we think drinking, smoking, cursing, adultery, etc. We Christians have levels of sin, but sin is missing the mark. *Sin* is not drinking, smoking etc., but it is *not* being born again. "For all have sinned and come short of the glory of God." (Romans 3:23)

"They answered and said unto him, you were altogether born in sins."(John 9:34)

> But the natural man receives not the things of the Spirit of God for they are foolishness unto him: neither can he know them, because they are spiritually discerned. But he that is spiritual judges all things yet he himself is judged of no man. For who hath known the mind of the Lord, that he may instruct him? But we have the mind of Christ. (1 Corinthians 2:14–16)

If it makes sense, it is not faith.

> It is the Spirit that quickens the flesh profits nothing: the words that I speak unto you, they are spirit and they are life. (John 6:63)

Verses 55 and 66 say, "From this time for many of His disciples went back and walked no more with Him."

Have you walked away?

> Know ye not that your body is the
> temple of the Holy Ghost which is in
> you, which ye have of God, and ye
> are not your own? For ye are bought
> with a price therefore glorify God in
> your body, and in your spirit, which
> are God's. (1 Corinthians 6:19–20)

The following verses speak to how to be born again.

> Being born again, not of corruptible
> seed, but incorruptible, by the Word
> of God, which lives and abides
> forever. Ye must be born again to
> enter the Kingdom of Heaven. (1
> Peter 1:23)

Marvel not that I said unto thee, Ye must be born
again. The wind blows where it will, and thou
hear the sound thereof, but canst not tell whence it
cometh, and whither it goes so is every one that is
born of the Spirit. (John 3:7–8)

Verse 12 says, "If I have told you earthly things, and
ye believe not, how shall ye believe, if I tell you of
heavenly things?"

Having abolished in his flesh the enmity, even the law of commandments contained in ordinance; for to make in himself of twain one new man, so making peace and that He might reconcile both unto God in one body by the cross, having slain the enmity thereby; And came and preached peace to you which were afar off, and to them that were nigh. For through Him we both have access by one Spirit unto the Father. (Ephesians 2:15–18)

That ye may be blameless and harmless, the sons of God, without rebuke, in the midst of a crooked and perverse nation, among who ye shine as lights in the world, holding forth the Word of life that I may rejoice in the day of Christ, that I have not run in vain, labor in vain, and if I be offered upon the sacrifice and service of your faith, I joy, and rejoice with you all. For the same cause also do ye joy, and rejoice with me. (Philippians 2:15–17)

> For in Christ Jesus neither circumcision avails anything, nor uncircumcision, but a new creature. (Galatians 6:15)

First John 3:9 tells us how to be born of God: "Whosoever is born of God doth not commit sin; for his seed remains in him and he cannot sin, because he is born of God.

New Covenant

Beloved, let us love one another for love is of God; and knows not God; for God is love. In this was manifested the love of God toward us, because that God sent His only Begotten Son into the world, that we might live through Him. Herein is love, not that we loved God, but that He loved us, and sent His Son to be the propitiation for our sins. Beloved, if God so loved us, we ought also to love one another. No man hath seen God at any time. If we love one another, God dwells in us, and His love is perfected in us. Hereby know we dwell in Him and He in us because He hath given us of His Spirit. And we have seen and do testify that the Father sent the Son to be the Savior of the world. Whosoever shall confess that Jesus is the Son of God, God dwells in him, and he in God.

And we have known and believed the love that God hath to us. God is love; and he that dwells in love dwells in God, and God in him. Herein is our love made perfect, that we may have boldness in the day of judgment: because as he is, so are we in this world. There is no fear in love; but perfect love casts out fear: because fear hath torment. He that fears cannot made perfect in love. We love him, because he first loved us. If a man say, I love God, and hates his brother, he is a liar: for he that loves not his brother whom he hath seen, how can he love God who he hath not seen? *And this commandment have we from him, that he who loveth God love his brother also.* (1 John 4, 7–21)

> Whosoever believeth that Jesus is the Christ is born of God and every one that loves him that begat, loves him also that is begotten of him. By this, we know that we love the children of God, when we love God, and keep His commandments (this is the commandment of love.) For this the love of God, that we keep His commandments; and His commandments are not grievous. For whatsoever is born of God overcomes the world and this the victory that

overcomes the world, even our faith.
(1 John 4:1–4, 18)

I know I am a son of God, but many do not. *We are made*: righteous, sanctified etc.

> For hath made him to be sin for us, who knew no sin; that we might be made the righteousness of God in Him. (2 Corinthians 5:21)

> And what agreement hath the temple of God with idols? For ye are the temple of the living God; as God hath said, I will dwell in them and walk in them; and I will be their God, and they shall be my people. And will be a Father unto you, and ye shall be my sons and daughters, says The Lord Almighty. (2 Corinthians 6:16, 18)

Born of Spirit

> But as many as received Him, to them gave him power to become the sons of God, even to them that believe on His name. Which were born not of blood, nor of the will of

the flesh, nor of the will of man, but of God. (John 1:12–13)

Jeremiah 31:31–34 is a prophecy—a new and better way in the future:

> Behold, the days come, says the Lord, that I will make a new covenant with the house of Israel, and with the house of Judah: Not according to the covenant that made with their fathers in the day that I took them out of the land of Egypt; which my covenant they brake, although I was and husband unto them, says the Lord; but this shall be the covenant that I will make with the house of Israel. After those days, says the Lord, I will put my law in their inward parts, and write it in their hearts; and will be their God, and they shall be my people.

> Therefore, if any man be in Christ, he is a new creature: old things are passed away; behold, all things are become new. And all things are of God, who hath reconciled us to

himself by Jesus Christ, and hath give to us the ministry of reconciliation. (2 Corinthians 5:17–21)

For Christ Jesus neither circumcision avails anything, nor uncircumcision, but a new creature. And as any as walk according to this rule, peace be on them and mercy and upon the Israel of God. (Galatians 6:15)

You Are Sealed

And that ye put on the new man, which after God is created in righteousness and true holiness. Wherefore putting away lying, speak every man truth with his neighbor: for we are members one of another. Be ye angry and sin not: let not the sun go down upon your wrath: Neither give place to the devil. Let him that stole steal no more: but rather let him labor, working with his hands the thing which is good, that he may have to give to him that needs. Let no corrupt communication proceed out of your mouth, but that which is

good to the use of edifying, that it
may minister grace unto the hearers.
And grieve not the Holy Spirit of
God, whereby ye are sealed unto
the day of redemption. (Ephesians
4:24–30)

After you are saved, you will sometimes stumble.
Don't think you need to start over again. Repent
of whatever you did and move forward, for the
knowledge you have gained to that point is not
forgotten. We sometimes get on a pity party.

Study about Peter as many times as he fell and
repented, just his shadow would heal the sick. We
sometimes think people in the Bible were perfect.
They were people like us, and many times the
stories are written to show us they had stumbles
and falls too.

Let's be sure we are new creatures. Search our
hearts, Lord. I pray, make us accountable to you,
Lord.

Also, put off these; anger,
wrath, malice, blasphemy, filthy
communication out of your mouth.
Lie not one to another, seeing that

ye have put off the old man with his deeds. And have put on the new man, which is renewed in knowledge after the image of Him that created him: Where there is neither Greek nor Jewish circumcision nor uncircumcision, Barbarian, Scythian, bond nor free: but Christ is all and in all. (Colossians 3:8–11)

For this is the blood of the New Testament, which is shed for many the remission of sins. (Matthew 26:28)

Remission means washed away, disappeared, a blank slate—as though it never happened

And He said unto them, this is my blood of the New Testament, which is shed for many. (Mark 14:24)

Likewise also the cup after supper saying, this cup is the New Testament in my blood, which is shed for you. (Luke 22:20)

Who also hath made us able minsters of the New Testament; not of the

letter [the Old Covenant], but of
the Spirit: for the letter kills, but the
Spirit giveth life. (2 Corinthians 3:6)

For finding fault with them, He says,
behold, the days come, says the Lord,
when I will make a New Covenant
with the house of Israel and with
the house of Judah: Not according
to the covenant that I made with
their fathers in the day when I took
them by the hand to lead them out
of the land of Egypt; Because they
continued not in my covenant, and
I regarded them not, says the Lord.
For this is the covenant that I will
make with the house of Israel after
those day says the Lord. I will put
my laws into their mind, and write
them in their hearts: and I will be to
them a God, and they shall be to me
a people: And they shall not teach
every man his neighbor, and every
man his brother, saying, Know the
Lord: for all shall know me, from
the least to the greatest. For I will
be merciful to their unrighteousness,
and their sins and their iniquities will

I remember no more. In that he says, a new covenant, He hath made the first old. Now that which decays and waxes old is ready to *vanish away*. (Hebrews 8:8–13)

Mediator

And for this because He is the mediator of the New Testament, that by means of death, for the redemption of the transgressions that were under the first testament, they which are called might receive the promise of eternal inheritance. (Hebrews 9:15)

And to Jesus the mediator of the New Covenant, and to the blood of sprinkling that speaks better things than that of Abel. (Hebrews 12:24)

New Way

By a new and living way, which He hath consecrated for us, through the veil, that is to say, His flesh. And having a high priest over the house of God. Let us draw near with a true heart in full assurance of faith, having our hearts sprinkled from an evil conscience, and our bodies washed with pure water. Let us hold fast the profession our faith without wavering (for he is faithful that promised [the devils seek to kill faith]). (Hebrews 10:20–23)

You have everything to gain and nothing to lose. All He asks is that you believe that He is. If you can believe that, then it is easy to see He died for you. I want to point out something here. Jesus said from now on you will ask *Me nothing.* But whatsoever you ask the Father in My name, He will give it to you. Asking amiss is a type of disobedience or rebellion.

The Bible is a guide that is like making ice cream. You must *do* what the recipe calls for, and you must read the recipe over and over again, for faith comes by hearing, not by having heard or by having studied or by having meditated or having gone to church three times this week, and you grow as the Word grows in you.

New Commandment

> A new commandment I give unto
> you, that ye love one another; as I
> have loved you, that ye also love one
> another. By this shall all men know
> that ye are my disciples, if ye have
> love one to another. (John 13:34–35)

For this New Covenant is *not* an extension
of the old commandments. What is this
commandment? To love others as ourselves. What
does the commandment include? *None* of the *old*
commandments for the *new* makes us *free*, giving
liberty and peace.

Law of *Love*

> How love acts-higher calling not a
> lesser covenant. A better promise.
> We are children of the Most High
> *God*. (1 Corinthians 13:4–8)

> Israel were servants, natural things
> are not things of the Spirit. (Galatians
> 3:26)

> Therefore, if any man be in Christ,
> he is a new creature: old things are

passed away; behold all things are become new. (2 Corinthians 5:17)

The new commandment is love shed abroad in our hearts.

> Charity (love) suffers long, and is kind, charity envies not; charity vaunts not itself, is not puffed up. Doth not behave itself unseemly, seeks not her own, is not easily provoked, thinks no evil; rejoices not in iniquity, but rejoices in the truth, bears all things; believeth all things, hopes all things, endures all things. (1 Corinthians 13:4–8)

Hope is a sure-fired, done deal, *not a wish! Yea!*

> Charity never fails, but whether there be prophecies, they shall fail; whether there be tongues, they shall cease; whether there be knowledge, it shall vanish away. (1 Corinthians 13:8)

> Knowing this, that the law is not made for a righteous man, but for the lawless and disobedient, for the

> ungodly and for sinner, for unholy
> and profane, for murderers of fathers
> and murderers of mothers, for man
> slayers, etc. (1 Timothy 1:9)

We should always ask the question, "What would love do?" God is love. He doesn't have love. It's one of His virtues. What would He do?

> For we know in part, and we prophecy
> in part. A new commandment I give
> unto you, that ye love one another:
> as I have loved you. That ye also
> love one another, by this shall all
> men know that ye are my disciples
> if ye have love one to another. (John
> 13:34–35)

CHAPTER 4

Powers, Principalities
and Ruler/Demons

*T*his chapter hopefully will inform you about demon spirits and how they may approach you. I want to make you aware that you are in charge and the largest demon can have no power over you unless you agree with him to do what he says. The authority comes from your covenant, God put all things under the feet of Jesus, and in Jesus's name you can put them there too.

(1 Corinthians 15:27).

Demons will often come to you through people. What they say is the reason it is so hurtful. Words are powerful, and that is the reason we shall be held accountable for every word. If you are an unbeliever and somehow are reading this, you must know that you will die someday. If you know this, it is written in the Bible. There may be some other stuff in there you may need to know, so you are not such an unbeliever after all.

To continue, many say the devil made them do it, but that's just not true. He can only be in one place at a time, and usually that is with kings and presidents trying to influence their decisions. Satan's kingdom is made up like an army. He is the head and has generals, colonels, and captains. It is regimented as a regular army. Many think they are being bothered by Satan when it's usually their own bad choices. What happens when you choose against right and go with the wrong? The only result that can happen is really bad stuff.

Ha! Guess what? The battle is between your ears. You consider what people say or do and don't realize the words can be distorted by imps in the air. What you hear is not really what they are saying. Thus, you get an attitude or pull out a pipe wrench, not thinking your life is about to change. This is not because Satan did anything but you just had to listen to those words. Read the Word, the good Word, the *Bible*.

That's the book for me. If you don't know what is in there or depend on a man to tell you, how do you know he knows correct? This is your life, and the devil is as a roaring lion *seeking* whom he can devour. *Aaahh*, that's the key he's seeking. In other words, he can't have the ones who know his tricks and ways. Like a computer, if someone is bullying you, block him or her. If that doesn't work, turn it off, and unplug. Go to the book and read and pray for your enemy. It is like pouring hot coals (Proverbs 25:22, Romans 12:20) on him and will be the hardest thing you will ever do. But the second time and after will be the easiest because once you let the Lord take care of your enemies and you see with your eyes what happens to them, you will want to pray because praying causes sin in a person to turn on him or her.

> Therefore if thine enemy hunger, feed him; if he thirst, give him drink: for in doing so thou shalt heap coals of fire on his head. (Romans 12:20)

> For you shall heap coals of fire upon his head, and the Lord shall reward thee. (Proverbs 25:22)

Our enemies are going to hell, and it is so heart rending when you understand hell is a long time. There is no end to it, no door to it, no bottom to it, no light in it, nothing to touch in it, just crying and gnashing of teeth. There are several ideas of how long hell is. Mount Everest, when a drop of rain falls on it, for a million years it will not have changed at all. When you have been there a million years, you will have just begun. It's really a long time. The book says the flames never cool off, bringing to my mind a piece of iron that is red hot and a paper or rope touches it and it immediately disappears. It's hotter than that. We have all heard of Satan. I guess he has gotten a lot of notoriety from a kid being told, "Do that and the devil will get you" to "The devil made me do it."

Some, you may even recognize, at least the way their followers worship them. The requirements of worshipping them are the same as far back as Babylon.

As today, a toy may be called a certain name at first, then twenty years later come back with a new name. The demons passed from Babylon to Ammon and to the Israelites with different names but the same murderous following. Baal plural was Baalim, whose wife was supposed to be

Ashteroth. Worshipping these evil gods was and is an abomination to God and anyone who looks upon it. They are pagans in the first form, and life means nothing to them. But getting humans to die or kill is the desire of these demons.

When the Israelites followed after these evil spirits to worship and build idols and have orgies in front of them, God's fury would come up into His face. Sometimes I think it may come up into my face too. (Not than I am close to God but human.) Why will come a little later on. These worshippers would go into the hills that they called high places and carve out faces of demons and/or animals on these living trees. They tended to worship earth, wind, and fire. The created things rather than the creator. The worshippers would dance and have music, all together sex—male and female, male with male, and female with female in the name of these so-called gods. They would build their idols of metal in the shape of beings with arms and head of animals. One was a woman with the tail of a fish. (Sound familiar?) Then they required the worshippers to heat up the metal with fire so hot they couldn't get very close to it. Then they would lay the babies on the arms of the idol as they cried and screamed and burned alive. The worshippers danced in fiesta and laughter and song. The smoke of fire and torment went up into God's nostrils. Another way they would build a fire would be to make a walkway to it and take sticks and whips and prod the children into the fire. As the children were screaming and crying, the drums would get louder and louder to drown out the noise so the revelers couldn't hear the struggles and horror of the children dying.

Dear God, help us. This spirit is still working in the world today remembering what Hitler did in Germany. It's still happening today in America, and we have grown deaf and numb to the cries of the children. We worry about air pollution, poor little animals, and poor little children. can see the ads in my mind's eye of the sad Indian, the poor one-eyed dog, the dirty kitten, and the dirty little child sitting in the dirt. No one remembers. It's not even a political issue anymore. The millions upon millions of babies about to be born are turned around in their mothers' wombs and forced to come out feet first. If that solution doesn't kill them, they stick scissors at the base of the skull and open and shut them till there is no more struggling. I guess that's a blessing? No more suffering? No one cared anyway. Oh God, forgive us of worshipping these *pagan* gods.

I put *please stop abortion* on my Facebook page, and I got *not one* like—*not one like, zero likes.*

I thought, *Is everyone dead? Did the rapture come and I got left?*

Okay, back to my book

Baal was a sun god worshipped by many countries by different names: Milcom, Moleck, Zeus. But they all required human sacrifice, bloodletting, and/or the drinking of blood—everything that is abhorred by God. Christians are the light of the world. Now is the time for our light to shine the brightest, the biggest, and the strongest we have ever shined before.

Stand up or *stay* home. Your decision is today.

Following is some more evidence of demonic activity. Witchcraft—did you know gossiping is the same as witchcraft? Wow, talk about bullying.

Divination, soothsaying, fortune telling, tarot cards, consulting with familiar spirits, communing with the dead, necromancy, Mother Earth, large trees, worshipping the devil, and drinking blood are examples of demonic activity. The blood belongs to God because the life is in the blood.

You know, the Bible told us thousands of years ago not to drink the blood. Now our scientists tell us the diseases we can catch. The Bible also tells us not to lay down with people of the same sex. We now see what calamity it can cause. I didn't say it; God did. Scientists have proven it.

There are a few things I want to say because I love you, but there are some lies that need to be corrected. Just because you're human does not make you my brother or sister.

Just because we happen to be the same color does not make you my brother or sister. Having the same Father makes me your brother or sister, no matter what nationality you may be or the color of your skin. My Father is God Almighty, and if He is your Father—which I pray He will be, if not now, after you read this book—that makes you my brother or sister. If He is not, your father is automatically Satan, because there is no other choice.

Marriage

If you are not comfortable with where you are in life, this will be an offensive chapter. I am only telling you what the Bible says so you have information. With information you can make good or bad decisions, but at least they are informed decisions. Okay? There is no need to get upset but turn on the tape player and record your reactions. That may be helpful. All sin is resisting the call of Jesus and actually, not accepting Him as your personal Savior and asking Him to come into your heart. But *all* sin can be washed away *only* by the *blood of Jesus*. These are sins of the flesh or body. I thought I was such a sinner that I could not be saved or forgiven, so one day, I said, "Self, you cannot be forgiven and certainly never will be forgiven, so why not just be a very good sinner?" That's what I began to be—a very good sinner. Now, listening to the errors made by people saying you can't do that, can't do this, just sent me reeling out of control. Many of you today are in the same boat. Jesus is our perfection. Groups are calling it *grace*. That's good, but it's just a fancy word for being washed cleaner than the laundry can get you. I'm listing these particular sins because they are an offense to your body. Better to marry than to burn in hell.

Women think if they are in love free sex is okay because it's *love*. First Corinthians 7:9 says, "I say therefore to the unmarried and widows, It is good for them if they abide even as I [single]. But if they cannot contain [stay out of bed], let them marry: for it is better to marry than to burn [in hell]."

With all the science we have out there today, it's almost like the soothsayer who was following Paul saying, "These are the men of the great God."

Being in love gives you no right to have sex or make love, as some would call it. It is simply using your body for basic recreation purposes that can have many fatal side effects, even ruining your already born children.

Loss of respect is the first one to show up in the very first morning. Then follows guilt, shame, sometimes sickness, or fatal sickness, then possible pregnancy, then thoughts of murdering that baby—so where did the love go?

Here are some consequences in alphabetical order:

Adultery is sexual unfaithfulness to one's spouse (Romans 1:18, Galatians 5:19).

Iniquity (Exodus 20:5) causes sin to be visited on children to the third and fourth generations.

Fornication—Acts 15:20 tells us to abstain from fornication, blood, and strangled meat. Fornication is all sex out of the marriage bed.

Adultery is conjugal infidelity—a man who has intercourse with a married or betrothed women or someone other than his spouse.

Iniquity is a wicked act of the worst kind. It is gross immorality, lawlessness, unrighteousness, and wickedness of the worst kind.

Fornication is voluntary sexual intercourse between two persons of the opposite sex, where one or both are unmarried. One thing you can say about my book if you sin, at least you know what to call it instead of love, heat, or lust.

Thank you and God bless you. Genesis 5:1–2 says that in the day that God created man (human), in the likeness of God made he him; male and female (man with a womb) created He them and called their name *Adam* in the day that they were created.

Wow, she wasn't named Eve at first, for God called *them* Adam or human.

Hadn't heard that before? Okay, let us continue about this marriage God set upon the earth, later giving instructions.

It is better to live alone and never marry if one can live without, as a eunuch. That puts God first in your life. But if you cannot restrain yourself from being involved with the other sex, it is better to marry. Do you wonder why He told us that? It's better to have a wife and be faithful than to lay down with a prostitute. *When* you have intercourse with a spouse (man if you're a woman, woman if you're a man), you become *one* with that person. *Can you see that?* It's important! Make note: God set marriage up to be two virgins marrying, and on the wedding night the hymen is broken. Blood flows, and it is a blood covenant between two persons (male and female).

They become one flesh. The child is their one flesh. Therefore, if you are a same-sex partner, you are welcome to call it anything you want. The Bible says it can't be covenant, can't be *one*, can't procreate. Remember, partner, *you're* responsible for the spiritual soul of your mate, so if you miss God or you are the cause of your mate missing God, you will be held more accountable in the end.

God bless.

Now you know the truth, and it *will* make you *free*.

I want to talk about this *oneness*. It is such an awesome, unbelievable thing. You always had the revelation of oneness being the mother and father equals oneness in the baby, right? When we accept God, He comes into our hearts and mixes His Spirit with our spirit man, and we become one with Him. I thought the oneness was mother plus father equals a baby.

Ponder this. Because we become married to God, we become one with Him. Think about a blender on the counter. Take a little of your DNA that seems like water and acts like water. Take a little of God's DNA that looks and acts like water, and put them both in the blender and stir.

Now, pour it through a strainer and separate it. *It's not possible.*

Yea! For *grace* more abundantly abounds than we can think or imagine.

> I rejoice greatly that I found of thy children walking in truth, as we have received a commandment from the Father. And now I beseech thee, lady, not as though I wrote a new commandment unto thee but that which we had *from the beginning*, that we love one another.

> And this is love that we walk after
> His commandments. This is the
> commandment, that, as ye have
> heard from the beginning, ye should
> walk in it. (2 John 4:5–6)

I would do you an injustice to end before I gave one more opportunity and plea to accept Christ as your personal Savior. Many people write books. If you have a copy of this book, it is certainly a miracle of God. You are certainly chosen of God, so what will you do with Jesus? I will end with this story I heard someone tell many years ago: A rich man had one son who went off to WWII and was killed. When the old man died, he left orders to sell all he had at the auction. The day of the auction came, and many people were waiting. The first item up for auction was an eight-by-ten photo of the son who was killed in action. The auctioneer said, "Who will give me fifty, fifty, a fifty-dollar bid?" Bidding went down for the painting of the son to a dollar. The old man's housekeeper bid one dollar. The auctioneer said, "Going, going, going, gone," and closed the auction. Everyone was confused as to why the bidding was over. He announced that the orders were, "Whoever buys the son gets it all."

What about you today? Will you pay a dollar for the Son and take it all? There is *no* charge. The Father's Son is free for the asking. Say *yes, yes, yes*

God bless you for reading my book, and may God bless your life in a special way. Please pray with me: Father, I realize You sent Your Son to die for me. Forgive me of all my past sins, and deliver me from the hands of the devil. I trust You to break the yoke of bondage and any curses or addictions that may try to present themselves against this word, that revelation knowledge will come and I will understand the meaning of this book, why it is written, and what God means it to say to me.

Come into my heart and live in me. I shall choose to give You glory and honor in my life the rest of my days. Thank You, Lord, for saving me. I will now walk in the kingdom of Your dear light, read Your Word, do Your Word, and listen to Your Word, be faithful to You, and allow You to do Your work in me.

I praise You, Lord, that I am saved, sanctified, and a born-again Christian on my way to heaven. I praise you that I am now an empty vessel to be filled by You, Father.

Amen!

Hallelujah. You are now in the kingdom of God and have become my brother or sister. Freed from every sin and problem, drugs, adultery, lust, prostitution, whatever was hanging over has been removed. When it comes at you say, "In the name of Jesus" out-loud till it leaves. As much as needed.

Healing=Sozo=is a Hebrew word meaning salvation, healing, peace, everything you'll ever need in life, you have now. Shalom is another word for all you need to walk through your problems. Remember Jesus is coming soon, keep looking up.

Amen, amen, and amen.

Printed in the United States
By Bookmasters